T0150089

The
SECRET
Art
of Selling
Insurance

STEP UP YOUR SALES GAME AND ATTRACT THE RIGHT CLIENTS

Ana-Maria Figueredo

THE SECRET ART OF SELLING INSURANCE
Step Up Your Sales Game and Attract the Right Clients

Difference Press, Washington, D.C., USA
© Ana-Maria Figueredo, 2021

ISBN: 978-1-68309-278-0

Cover Design: Nakita Duncan
Interior Book Design: Anna Zubrytska
Editing: Moriah Howell
Author Photo Credit: Lynn Parks

DIFFERENCE
P R E S S

ADVANCE PRAISE

As a newcomer into the Insurance industry this book could have not come out at a better time. *The Secret Art of Selling Insurance* is genuinely written with all levels of sales experiences in mind. Whether a newcomer or a top producer with years of experience this book will deliver the understanding of building and growing your business.

~ Lilia Caballero/Licensed Independent Insurance Producer

I think it's very well done by blending the author's experiences with well-known historic personalities. This creates links that makes it easier to remember new ideas.

~ Gabriel Brakha, MBA, President of
Insurance Consultants International

I am sharing this book with all my agents, I am sure that will be easy for them to find clients and close the deal. The "meet your customer in a non-invasive manner" is a very powerful concept. This is an excellent book.

~ *Victor Pradenas, Sales Manager*

I'm blown away by Ana-Maria Figueredo's creative, relational approach to insurance sales! I can see I have avoided salespeople (especially insurance) in a way I used to avoid the homeless... but reading your book makes me see salespeople as humans. What a gift!

– Robin Winn, bestselling author of
Understanding Your Clients through Human Design

For Bill

TABLE OF CONTENTS

FOREWORD

When one has the esteemed pleasure of serving as a business coach, it is an honor to observe the student become the teacher. Ana Maria Figueredo is that student who now holds the position of sales coach. What you are about to read is not only based on what Ana Maria has experienced, but what she has learned to now successfully teach. As many leaders will tell you, doing and teaching are two entirely different things and as has likely been *your* experience, until you are able to teach your talents to those you have the privilege of leading, you aren't really leading much of anything.

Ana Maria is now your sales coach through the book you now hold in your hand. In *The Secret Art of Selling Insurance*, she spells out the sales process, goes step by step, and propels you into the land of complete and utter success. Whether you sell actual insurance or simply need to sell your ideas to the clients of your business, you are truly in for a treat and some powerful, positive results. As she speaks to you through these pages, much as she would in a sales conversation, you and she will develop a relationship and she will become your guide on the side for the areas of sales that most won't even touch. From honing your reputation, to uncovering your competitive edge, to finding real decision makers and removing what you may now see as barriers, you'll be excited about your results no matter who you work with or what product you sell.

It is the same way in which Ana Maria and I got to know each other. We had a conversation. We developed a relationship. My Executive Coaching skills were a good fit for her needs at that time in her life. She'd never hired a coach before, much like you will likely encounter clients who are first time buyers. I'd never coaching Ana Maria before we got started, but I can tell you that in fifteen years of coaching leaders of all levels, she still stands out as a top performer. We're both straight shooters, she and I. We've both authored numerous books and we've both lived the wisdom we share with others. And while I might *Make Difficult People Disappear*, Ana Maria will make your next promotion and sales quota appear and reappear, time and time again. Buckle up, get ready, and by all means, dive right in!

Monica Wofford
CSP CEO | Contagious Companies, Inc.
www.ContagiousCompanies.com

Chapter 1

IS THERE A SECRET ART TO SELLING ENOUGH TO GET A PROMOTION?

I've missed more than 9,000 shots in my career. I've lost almost 300 games. Twenty-six times, I've been trusted to take the game winning shot and missed. I've failed over and over and over again in my life.

~ Michael Jordan ~

The writing of this book was inspired by a particular person who upon meeting me said, "Everyone knows you, and they love you, too! How did you do that?" My answer was that I use my secret art of sales. This person continued, "I need to know how to sell more insurance effectively, or I will lose my chance at a promotion."

Immediately, I understood this angst. It is the same sweaty-palmed fret a gambler has while putting everything at stake. Exactly that, sales is a gamble for most people. Although sales can be thrilling, and luck can definitely play a role, the professional salesperson does not rely on luck or hope. A real salesperson has a strategy.

Throughout my years as a sales professional, I've seen a lot of people either sink or swim. It makes you wonder what differentiates one from another. You can have two people equally smart and talented, just as charming, and know nothing terribly definitive about whether they will succeed or not. One will sell everything off the shelf, for example, and the other will not even get one interested buyer.

Why is that?

Well, there's a lot involved. Some people are natural predators and will force the sale out of a person with a persistence that is almost overwhelming. Others are very charming and can virtually hypnotize the buyer. The really successful sales professional has a method to engage the buyer, and makes the right fit for the need happen. This is the person who makes sales an artform.

Those who fail have no real interest in selling in the first place. They might want to make a living and think sales are easy. Sales positions tend to be easy on the body and are housed in comfortable working locations. The promise of a lucrative career can attract a lot of people to a sales position; however, it takes the right attitude and enthusiasm to close a sale. Otherwise, the non-sale conversation becomes a source of information about a product. A position in copywriting or customer service is a better fit for a non-salesperson.

Tension and pressure to sell are a deathtrap! Do not succumb to or enforce threats to your sales as an individual or as a leader. The sales will come naturally and can't be forced. Pressure to sell can be as deadly to a sale as pressure to buy. It never ends well. Plus, you risk a chargeback or return on the product. Clean sales make for repeat business and referrals. This is our goal.

This book is for the person who wants to be a serious sales professional and desires to be promoted to the highest level possible in the sales arena. Everything I do and how I learned it is in this book. Now, mind you, it spans decades of learning, observing, successes, and failures. I will detail how to pursue this goal step by step and become the go-to sales professional for your industry. The secret to this is building significant relationships and creating the reputation that will attract your customers to you without you knowing anything about them! Everyone knows a doctor, a lawyer, or a restaurant that people swear by, and that can be you!

The problem is that you've got a great product with great features and benefits, but no one is buying. How can you change that radically? I've known of many excellent products that couldn't even be given away, much less sold. It can get you to the brink of losing your business. Then you become someone at the mercy of investors or loans to keep you afloat.

If you are a good listener and learn my process, you will not succumb to that fate. However, you must at once let go of the biggest obstacle, which is believing you are right. The customer is always right. The customer's goals are what we are aiming for with every single sale. If you are not the right fit, let it go and part as friends. Better yet, suggest the right solution and guide the customer to where to find it. You will ensure having lots of friends in your industry and a job opening if something happens to the product or company you represent.

Generosity is also a great sales magnet. Always be generous with your potential client as well as your competition. Share information freely. Good information is addictive, and like good gossip or good reviews, it spreads. Plus, everyone wants to know the source. Be a source of good information to everyone. Give it away freely! I will address how to spread your knowledge and expertise to crowds of people.

Products and companies will come and go, but your relationships will stay if you nurture them properly. As a dear friend of mine once said, "Darling, it's not who you know, it's who knows you!" I believe this to be true in many respects and certainly in sales.

In many sales organizations, the highest promotion is getting to manage other people. You nurture and feed them until they can hunt on their own, and it will bring more returns to your wallet. Although this is not a book about management, this is a how to become such a great source of business, it will be enough to get a promotion and supply your own team to work with. Teach all your team members these techniques, and you will grow exponentially. If your book of business grows as it should, you will need to hire people to help you with the workload. You will definitely get that promotion!

I invite you to explore the endless opportunities and supply of businesses available to you. The only limit is in your imagination. If you need to expand your product line, hire people, get a larger location, then all the better. Prosperity brings growth and change, there is nothing to fear. It won't happen until it's necessary.

So, welcome to the world of sales and the secrets to building an ample, healthy book of business. Remember, this is fun, because you decide who you will do business with! You will hand-pick your clients and learn to find their sweet spot. Once you are known as a problem solver with the right solutions, you will have a following and not have to hustle as much. However, you will enjoy every minute if you are a true sales professional.

Also note that if you are having fun, you will be a natural business magnet. People not only buy from who they like, they buy from people who make it enjoyable. Take your adventure pills and enjoy the ride!

Let's have fun!

Chapter 2

THE EVOLUTION OF EXPERIENCES AND KNOWLEDGE INTO SALES CONVERSION

My journey into sales was not easy. When I was still a classroom teacher, my former husband told me that I'd be good at sales. I was deeply insulted, as if he'd suggested I'd be a good serial killer or con artist! I wanted to be an artist, a writer, and I loved teaching high school kids. Back then, teaching was an art and not a drill-and-kill machine for maximizing performance with standardized tests. I got to teach theater, world literature, and creative writing. I wore tie-dye dresses and Birkenstocks or jeans with cool t-shirts and enjoyed myself tremendously.

Once I left teaching students to teach teachers, it was more of a corporate world. I was hired by the largest educational software retailer in the country and traveled to over thirty-eight states, Puerto Rico, and Hawaii, showing teachers how to implement different software programs into their existing curriculum. Although they were adults, I still taught people how to be creative and have fun. My staff development trainings were so successful that I was asked to train new sales team members when they were hired. I specifically taught them features and benefits, not implementation. Many of the salespeople would request to have me present the products so they could really get school districts excited and ready to buy. The CEO of the company started sending me out to independent sales organizations and training them. That's when the first passion for sales hit me. I was working in Memphis, Tennessee with an African American sales team who were so generous, hospitable, and shared so much of their culture and knowledge with me that I was hooked. Not only did I want to pursue sales, I wanted to be independent and use my skills on my terms.

My whole attitude towards sales had changed. I realized selling could be done on my own terms and with integrity. Since then, I measure my success by the respect and loyalty of my customers, not the size of my bank account. I have a true following that will never leave me, because I know what they need and will listen to how that changes due to whatever circumstances arise.

Shortly after, I started my first company specializing in staff development, creating websites, and putting together home offices. It was an instant success, and all the companies who knew my work hired me before I even started taking business calls. I learned how to network and pursue small businesses in my area for a variety of technology-related services. I travelled as much or more than I had as an employee. It was fun, and it was exhilarating. I presented in every national conference in my field of educational technology and earned more business each time.

Then, one of the largest educational software companies in the country offered me an executive manager position for the southeastern states, spanning from Florida up to North Carolina and as far west as Texas. My sales career was well on its way, and there was no turning back! For the next ten years or so, I worked the same territory with similar project-based educational technology tools and built a great book of business.

Then in my personal life, my aging parents influenced my decision to stay home and make a living locally. They were both growing more frail by the minute and approaching the end of their lives. I wanted to be available to them and keep them in high spirits. So, I started consulting local businesses and entrepreneurs, ran a networking group for professional women, and eventually got into the insurance industry. Each venture required building a new book of business and hustling new products. I did so fearlessly, because I knew how to do it and had a great deal of fun growing each one. Many of my former clients remain my friends and keep in touch via social media.

To this day, everything I've ever done is used in my sales approach. I tell relatable stories about my childhood, my education, my travels, the challenges and turmoil of being alive, family stories, pet stories, etc. It all becomes part of my story and my sales pitch. We are all alive and sharing a human experience, and everyone likes knowing they aren't alone.

The secret is being a good storyteller and drawing your audience into what you are talking about. People buy ideas and concepts, not stuff. So, it doesn't matter if you are selling clothes, cars, jewelry, gadgets, services, or insurance. The concept behind what you are selling will close the deal. Your stories about life, experiences, and observations will help you do that. I will teach you to transform your mind into a sales-conversion machine by truly connecting with your customer.

The secret is also being real. I will repeat this over and over again: people buy from people they like. Having a natural and easy-going approach is essential in gaining trust and respect from your audience. Have a higher goal and purpose to what you are doing. Find meaning in your daily communications and let them enrich both your life and the lives of all those around you.

The secret is to never stop evolving as a human being and to gain more compassion with everyone you meet. Learn their stories and build a future of stories together. Those people are a fountain of success stories for you. Both you and they will spread that success organically. Make the commitment to grow with your customers. It becomes a deep-rooted relationship and symbiotic in that you both feed each other!

The secret to your success is *you!*

It has become second nature to me, and it will become second nature to you if you follow my method and secret to the art of selling.

Chapter 3

WORK SMARTER, NOT HARDER

Give me six hours to chop down a tree and I will spend the first four hours sharpening the axe.

~ Abraham Lincoln ~

My intention is to show you how to work smarter and not harder. Life is meant to be enjoyed, and working all the time will not satisfy the more important needs you have. However, my method is enjoyable and will prove to be a very pleasant way to do business both for you and those around you.

Not that this is going to be easy. Most things worth doing aren't easy. It will become second nature with time if you get the hang of it. It is like getting your sea legs when on a boat or learning to make scrambled eggs. It takes practice.

We are going to explore how to make the right connections and execute the perfect sale. It seems simple enough, but it takes some research and depth of understanding. When I had a quarter of the United States as my sales territory, it would have taken years to visit and serve every school district. I had to work smart and be efficient with my time and resources. It is the best way to be successful in both sales and life.

There is an underlying fact all salespeople must determine early on. Does the sales target have the right DNA? Does the Desire exist? Does the target Need your product? Does the target have the Ability to pay? Determining these attributes are the most difficult things before executing a sale. It is the prework. It takes time and patience.

Then, it's just a matter of focusing on the prospective customers with the right DNA! Who are they? Who do you like and want to deal with? Create lists and design the prototype/archetype of that glorious persona who will be an absolute pleasure to deal with!

Let's find them! Where do they live, eat, play, and work? How can you mingle with them? Do you already know them or have access to them? Is there an association they belong to? What is the plan of attack? What do you feel comfortable with?

This part is a lot like dating. It's terrifying for a lot of people. You have to get out there and be judged by strangers who don't really know you. Guess what? They don't have to know you. You need to know them, their goals, and how you can help them achieve them. It's not about you! You are merely the problem solver!

Once you let go of it being personal and understand what your role is, the easier it will get. You are a vehicle of a larger purpose, and it isn't personal. The rejection isn't personal when it isn't the right fit. The successful sale is personal because you orchestrated it!

What I'll show you is *how* to orchestrate it! First you need to get in front of these prospects and make a deep and profound impression. Then, deliver your pitch. After that, prove it can be done, if necessary. Work your way to the decision makers and money spenders effortlessly. Develop those relationships. Make it effortless and fun for everyone involved.

Chapter 4

IDENTIFY YOUR CUSTOMER

Sales is a lot like stalking! Get an idea of who you want as a customer, create an excuse to approach them, and get their attention. It seems a bit creepy, but there's a fine line between selling like a creep and selling gracefully. That's why sales as a profession gets a bad reputation. Many people say they aren't salespeople with a sense of pride and distinction, as if it were below them. Guess what? It isn't! Everything in life is sales driven. We are all sellers and buyers, and that's what makes the world go around! I love my profession, so that really helps with becoming good at it. Practice telling people you are a salesperson with pride! It is the oldest profession in the world, and everyone needs it!

Now, you might say to me, "I thought prostitution is the oldest profession!" You are right! It is, and it is also sales! It will always be number one, because successful prostitutes know the most important rule in having a satisfied and generous buyer. The secret to a salesperson's success (regardless of the product) is giving the customer what they want. A successful courtesan gives customers exactly what they asked for and, in many cases, it isn't even sex.

Accordingly, your first step is the following: identify your customer. Who wants your product?

Come up with the reason you think and would pitch to anyone that would need your product.

For example, in the insurance world, you could say everyone needs insurance. You are right. "Everyone needs insurance" is a valid statement, because no matter how much money or success you might have, financial protection is a great reason to get insurance. No one wants to go bankrupt if they get sick. But who is going to value that pitch?

I would focus on small business owners. They can't afford to lose their income, assets, or go bankrupt. Small business owners usually have families too. They don't want their kids or spouse to not have the comfort of a home, healthcare, and everything else they need to survive. If they have partners, they don't want an illness to be the end of the support they need. I could go on and on as to why these people are a perfect fit.

However, there are a lot of business owners out there. Where should you start? The easiest step is to approach the people you already know and do business with. They're your drycleaner, your grocer, your mechanic, your hairdresser, your dentist, etc. I used to insure everyone in my hairdresser's salon, dentist office, and favorite restaurants. They trusted me because they already knew me.

When I first went into sales, I used the yellow pages and let my fingers do the walking. Now you have the internet, which makes everything so much easier. Just do a search on small businesses in any desired area code, and you will have your first batch of prospects at your disposal. Save your copy on a spreadsheet or Word document where you can write notes and keep track of your progress. You are now one step closer to success!

Take a good look at your list and see if anyone stands out or maybe you know them personally. Look up their websites and learn more about them. If they are part of a larger corporation or a chain, eliminate them. We are going after low-hanging fruit right now, not the big leagues. Unless, like many restaurant chains and supermarkets, some do not offer group insurance. So, think about it or investigate a little closer.

You have your list and a good idea of who and what each business is about. Now what? Ask yourself what your strongest form of communication is. Are you a great phone person, charming in person, or a master at marketing via email? How will you make your first move? If you can, practice your approach on a friend or someone you aren't trying to sell to. See their body language and tone when they react. Are they receptive or repelled? The best way to know if you are doing well is when they immediately think of someone who needs your product.

What does your customer need? Once you start speaking to people you've identified as potential customers, the most important part of the conversation is going to be determining what you will sell to them, if you will sell them anything at all. Don't let this be your primary focus in the conversation, because it will make you seem like a creepy salesperson. Your focus is going to be on getting to know your potential customer.

Know enough about the business and what the goals and focus are before you initiate any contact. Have an intelligent conversation where you get to know the person a little more in depth and take a genuine interest in something you have in common. Make that connection. People buy from people they like. You might not even have the best product in the world, but if you are nice and likable, you can sell virtually anything. Sometimes if the person likes you enough, they will find a way to give you their business.

"What else do you sell?" or "Do you sell life insurance?" are dead giveaways that they are digging to give you their business. The real question they are asking is, "Do you have something I can buy from you?"

Make sure they buy what they need and don't fall off your book of business. A clean sale is a good sale, and you want the repeat business and referrals for more than one crummy commission. Professional charmers do well with numbers, but if half the sales they get on the board fall off, the money falls off too!

When I was in educational sales, I would study each school district's mission and goals for the year. In doing so, I'd see how my product aligned with their goals and how I could enhance the work they had ahead of them. Once I determined who and how I would contact my potential client, it was a matter of discussing their vision. By doing so, I created a partnership with them with a common goal. They would succeed with their mission, and my product would enable them to accomplish it with my guidance or supervision.

Again, I stress the importance of identifying the need of your customer. If you are selling insurance to a self-employed person with small school aged children, the kids will need proof of insurance to attend school. Look for a meaningful need that must be solved. Find out as much as you can about the person and what they think. Once, I recommended a fishing charter boat captain get some accident insurance. She declined and only bought basic health insurance. A week later she slipped, fell, and broke her nose. She called me and bought that extra coverage after realizing how much money she would have saved for a tiny monthly investment. She also referred me to all her captain friends, because I never pushed her.

If you listen carefully and know your products and how to place them, you will win the respect of your clients. I travelled to meet a school administrator for lunch one afternoon to pitch my educational product. She seemed really distressed and worried about something; it was distracting her from our conversation. I was direct and asked her what was going on. She told me about a video editing software company leaving the educational market and really messing up all of her ongoing projects districtwide. I quickly recommended a similar product owned and designed by a friend of mine in the software industry. It ended up not only solving her problem, it also provided my friend with a quarter million-dollar sale. I won two friends for life: a future loyal client and a pending job offer for years to come. Superficially, it was a waste of time, gas, and a non-sale. With time, it helped open many doors to new school districts, because I became known as a problem solver and solution provider.

Oh, incidentally, that $250,000 sale closed without ever demonstrating the product. The customer ordered it because my description fit her need. It was effortless.

The importance of identifying your customer is that, for whatever reason you selected that particular type of person, values, or profession, you will actually enjoy working. You are choosing the demographic you want to spend most of your day with, pursue, and grow with. It really defines who you want to be and how you want to be known. This is vital for the next step of getting in the door to meet your prospect.

Chapter 5

MEET YOUR CUSTOMER IN A NON-INVASIVE MANNER

You now have your list of potential clients. But how do you meet them? Is it awkward? Do you say, "Hi, my name is Ana-Maria, and I want you to buy some insurance?" You could, but let me discuss a more effective method.

When I was about to start my first business, I saw a woman walking down the street. She seemed really cool and put-together. I loved her attitude and how she was dressed, and I wanted to know more about what she was about. I caught up with her and said, "Hi, I want to know everything about you. Please start wherever you feel comfortable!" She smiled and told me I was delightful. She gave me her card and said, "Call me and we can have coffee!" She proceeded to walk away.

I had my "a-ha!" moment! Coffee! This was before Starbucks was even in my city, mind you. I think this was back in the early 90s, before meeting at Starbucks was such a phenomenon. An invitation to a public cup of coffee is the safest invitation there is! That's why online daters overuse it. There's no commitment.

Call those business owners and invite them to a cup of coffee. Tell them you are new to the neighborhood and just started a business, or that you noticed they were new to the area. Make it a simple meet-and-greet, as if you were going on a first date. No pressure, no pitch, no problem. Of course, if they need your services when you say what you do, then get that business!

With time, you will become someone who knows a lot of key people, and, better yet, they know you. Feel free to do a little matchmaking to appear more attractive. If you know a good shoe repair guy and someone complains about their feet, give them a heads up. If someone just got into an accident and needs a lawyer, it just so happens you know a wonderful attorney. Get the picture? Be useful and informed. It also proves you are listening and not just out for yourself. Like the quarter million dollar deal I mentioned in the last chapter, the good deed comes back to you a hundred-fold!

Next, emails are good because they can contain your business card and links to your website and social media.

However, emails are not always read, and everyone gets hundreds of emails saturating their servers every day. Make sure you have something catchy that makes yours stand out. Have an interesting meme, picture, or subject that calls attention to you in a sincere and fun way. Don't have all your communication be sales driven; share some inspirational quotes, beautiful pictures, and pictures of your pets or kids. Be human.

Then, the message in the email should be very clear and to the point. Every few years, I would change companies or what I was focusing on with insurance. I'd send out a clear update email saying it was an update on what I was doing on the subject line. Then I'd have a clear description written out in both English and Spanish for my existing book of business. It is amazing how many people respond or call to discuss myriad things. It is a simple reminder that you are still out there and haven't forgotten that they once were your esteemed clients.

Don't overuse or flood your prospects with emails. Give them a clear choice of how to *opt out*. Make sure your communications are meaningful. If you have a newsletter or email campaign, make the invitation clear, and, again, let them reject it graciously. Emails really annoy people because there is so much useless information bombarding them that they miss important messages all the time!

If you have a highly visual image to share, get a printer to create a mail campaign for you! If it isn't visual, mail might be a waste of time. Most people toss anything that isn't a bill immediately without even giving mail a chance. You need to have something radically special to make that work. Choosing the right printer and mail campaign is key. Smaller printing offices offer more personalized service and are more expensive while larger companies are more budget conscious, but not as detail oriented. I like the more personal relationship. Also, meeting printers and brainstorming with them could earn you some unexpected business!

If your budget permits, events are huge! I love the idea of potential clients coming to me, and potential clients love being courted. It makes the contacts you reach feel special and important. Everybody loves a lunch and learn. You can provide lunch to a large office and give a presentation. You can rent a space and create a marketed event to showcase your products. You can buy a table or booth at trade shows. These are all extremely effective ways of meeting people and getting introduced to them.

Realtor offices are great spots for lunch and learns. Find out when the monthly meeting is being held and cater lunch with the promise of giving you at least fifteen minutes to speak. Have packets ready with information and some goodies. Offer to stick around and meet everyone individually to quote them without any obligation to buy.

Many restaurants have private meeting rooms, and there are also social clubs that have different sized meeting rooms with catering services. Get to know what is out there, the pricing, and the accessibility to potential clients. Then your prospects can all come to you for a continental breakfast before going to work, or a nice warm lunch to see a full presentation about your products. Have a gift or door prize to capitalize on the element of surprise and appreciation felt by all. Also, follow up with thank you notes or emails plus an invitation to meet one-on-one.

Local county and city networking opportunities are another great way to meet potential clients. Get a table or booth, some candy and small gifts ready, and schmooze with every person as they walk by. Have a fishbowl for cards promising a special gift or consultation. Draw the participants in with something different like a beautiful centerpiece you can gift to someone at the end of the day. Meet all the other vendors and make sure you let what you do be known to all.

Once the relationship and trust grows, you can start to subtly ask who makes decisions about insurance in the company. Many times, the prospect will automatically advise you on how to approach the decision makers, but make a simple and direct request on how to move forward. It is completely acceptable and honest.

Chapter 6

FINDING THE QUALIFIED BUYERS AND DECISION MAKERS

You are meeting people, making connections, and having fun, but where's the money? Who decides what or when to buy? Who has the money to buy? What is the financial situation of your potential client?

The first thing you have to erase from your mind is any assumption about a person's bank account balance. Or, in other words, "Get your hand out of your client's pocketbook or wallet!" When people really feel they want or need something, the money appears. There are family members, friends, lovers, and side hustles that provide for things outside the IRS, payroll, or expected income bracket. Don't judge; just sell.

I'll never forget a beautiful woman who walked into my office one day. She had designer clothes on from head to toe and was perfectly groomed and manicured to perfection. She sat down and asked for insurance with determination to buy. I asked her for her basic information including her address. She lived in a penthouse in a trendy neighborhood, was single, and lived alone. So, I asked her for her income. She didn't work. I asked her how she paid for things and she smiled as she took out her checkbook. I stopped asking questions and signed her up. It was none of my business!

Focus on the goals your customer has and what it takes to achieve them. Don't go high end or low end; go directly to the best solution. The best solution is not necessarily the most expensive! That's what is going to win your business and ongoing respect.

There were many times I had people accustomed to the best ask me for the top of the line insurance I sold. I often responded, "You want the same insurance I sold a paraplegic bound to a wheelchair?" The customer looked confused. I'd answer, "Why do you want insurance and what to you want it to cover? I promise I'll get you exactly what you need!" The reason behind this was to make it clear to the customer I was not taking anyone for a ride. The most expensive is not going to make a difference to me as a salesperson if it isn't the right fit. Many times, people accustomed to the best won't care and will buy it anyway, but everyone appreciates a good sales professional. They will come back to you because you refused to rip them off and so will their friends, I assure you of this!

Next, you should know if the person is married or not before pitching to them. Ask if there is anyone else needing insurance in their household and also know if anyone else needs to hear about the solution you have. Be aware of what needs the additional adults or children may have. Everyone in the same house might not need the same solution. If you are the one to express the need to have an additional decisionmaker present, you will not only save time, but you will put the potential buyer at ease about getting a buy-in from a spouse. Many times, the person will insist they can move forward to make all the decisions and pay. Perfect – move forward.

If you are dealing with a company, it might get a little complicated. Be straightforward and ask, "Who makes the purchasing decisions in your company?" or "Are there any decision makers that need to see or hear this?" Let the person in front of you be your coach through the selling process. Also, get a strong idea of how many presentations it will take to close. It can be a long process if you are talking large numbers. It might be easier to have a lunch and learn or set up a day to meet with various people in the same office or building.

At some point, you have to get down and dirty to talk about money. I've encountered many salespeople who let this be their downfall. Letting money get in your way of a sale has everything to do with your relationship with money, not theirs! Explore that issue if you have trouble asking for a form of payment. Do you start to avoid working when this happens? Do you feel guilty about taking people's money? It can define the difference between being a top producer and an average salesperson. You might not lose your job, but why survive when you can thrive?

Asking for money is a huge obstacle for many businesspeople. It is the heart and soul of being a salesperson, so this is a touchy subject. If you aren't okay with asking for a payment, then you might not be cut out for this line of work. No one ever went into a car lot and drove off with a vehicle without paying for it. Money is a simple exchange of energy put out as an effort towards change. Anything you want in life will cost you something physical, emotional, or spiritual. If you can't ask for a payment naturally, you can't sell.

Think of the cause and effect resulting in making a change. If I want to go from point A to B, I must do X. If you want financial security, you must buy this product to protect you. If you want to pay less at a moment of crisis, you pay gradually before a crisis occurs, therefore a crisis will have less of an impact on you financially.

There is a point in every sales conversation where I feel it is the right moment to ask for a credit card. It comes at a delightful pause when everything necessary has been discussed, and it's just time to move on. A simple, "What form of payment will we be using today?" can be asked as naturally as "What will you have for lunch?" It isn't a big deal. Just ask.

"Are you ready to get started today?" or "How soon do you need this?" are assumptive closes that can be thrown into the conversation at some time before the close as well. Make sure you are on the same page as to why you are talking. This is the moment when you make it clear you mean business and are not socializing.

If the person hesitates, it could be one of two things: either they have no funds, or they aren't convinced you have the right solution. Start over. Explain why the product is what they need. Say you don't understand why they are not taking advantage of this moment. Offer to set up a payment in the future but take all the necessary information and application now.

Some buyers are simply indecisive! You might be facing someone afraid of spending money or afraid of making a commitment. Make sure the value of the product is evident and dig to find out what is creating hesitation. Keep control of the situation and decide for them. Tell them what the best and worst possible situations are if they act now. Allow them time to shop around if they want to, but warn them, they will just return for more of what you got. If it isn't the right fit, let them go. Actually, tell them exactly why you refuse to sell to them! I've won countless accounts pushing away at the right moment. However, trust your gut. It might not be worth the sale for all the hassle.

One year during an open enrollment for Obamacare, I was sitting at a local drugstore with a tablet giving people quotes on subsidies. One man sat with me and kept asking me to check again with a different yearly income level. After the third try and a long line of serious insurance-seekers waiting, I gave him my card and told him to call me once he decided what his income truly was. Yes, I lost a possible sale, but that man was not going to be able to prove his income, and I was inviting an audit from the CMS. No way! Some business isn't worth the grief, and there were plenty of people needing my assistance.

Now that you have your potential client's attention and willingness to pay, a little buyer's remorse might arise. The customer might wonder if your product is the right choice or wonder why that product is the best option. It reminds me of my first interview for a sales position where the hiring manager asked me why I thought I'd be a successful candidate having no experience in sales. Basically, I was asked, "Why should I hire you?" I responded that I could get forty-eight teenagers to read Shakespeare, and if that isn't sales, I don't know what persuasion is. I was bold and edgy with that answer, as you will learn to be.

Chapter 7

HONING YOUR COMPETITIVE EDGE

Competition is good. It keeps you hungry and on your toes! Embrace it! Make sure your product is just as good, if not better. Never sell anything below the level you feel is right. It is going to get to you and mess with your flow. Being the most expensive is okay, too. I'll never forget a woman I worked with that compared our educational product to retail shopping. "Honey, we are Neiman Marcus, not Walmart!" She delivered that statement with a natural diva air that was both wonderful and true! If your product is more like Walmart, that's good, too! There is space for all the stores, and it's imperative that you offer affordable solutions to all needing your help. Choose your product wisely and stand behind it.

It is your responsibility to wisely select the products you represent. It is your trademark, reputation, and integrity on the line here. Personally, I won't represent local companies, only national ones with very few exceptions. The financials of the company are very important as well as their ability and willingness to pay claims. You are the face of the company for your clients. Don't let them down.

In fact, your customer isn't only buying your product, your customer is buying you! You are the number one product you sell, so be mindful of what you put out there. Good grooming, manicures, pedicures, and your fashion statement are all part of the package – as is your perfume. It doesn't matter if they see you or not; it is your attitude that will come forth and show itself. Too much can also work against you. Getting too corporate when visiting a person's home or hanging out at a local pharmacy might make you standoffish. Find a way to be attractive and relatable to your customer. Remember, it isn't personal – you are your best product!

Know your competition. Research them, the pricing, the financial strength of the company, the staff, the people in your position directly going after the same business. Many times, you can create strategic alliances because your products have different strengths. I've made many friends out of my competitors, and it always served to my advantage. No product or company has everything, so it's good to send your competition some business when it is a better fit for your customer. You never know who your best ally will be! Plus, you won't lose that customer. They are bound to return to you when you work at that high level of integrity. Surely, their friends and family will hear about you too.

There are certain products I simply will not sell. However, there is a market for these products and many people love them. I have a competitor who sells these products and we exchange referrals on a regular basis. It is a rewarding relationship and demonstrates our open mindedness to alternative solutions for the most important outcome: customer satisfaction.

Never speak poorly of a competitor, either. You might discuss how you only know your own product, not anyone else's, with your customer. It's okay to lie about it. Or, you can quote a famous actress I often quote when cornered about discussing my competition: "I find it much more interesting to speak well about myself than badly about others!" Of course, she was talking about famous lovers she had been linked to, but she kept a tasteful mystery about her.

Don't be afraid to rate your product. Perhaps you don't have the top selling product. Know why someone would choose yours over the top of the line. Is it the price point, durability, maintenance, etc.? Isn't there always a reason why a product was created, and isn't there always an audience it was created for? If it is the high end, boast about it without worries. There's a reason that the number one *is* number one, and the price to be there has been paid for you. Just pave your way to keeping it there with grace. In many cases, the products and companies you represent are so strong, you just make sure you keep true to the messaging and value statements they have already established.

In Florida, I sell a particular product which I know is the best. The company has been around for over a hundred years, and it has an impeccable reputation. That is nice, but the customer wants to know what makes it good for their needs. Well, when push comes to shove, this company has the economic funding to pay the bills. When the crisis no one expects arrives, there won't be any questions or proof of loss necessary – this company will step up and do what is required. Do you realize how good it feels to provide this type of coverage? You become the hero.

The reason the person interested in purchasing your product chose you is because you have either won their trust or goodwill. It isn't anything else. Most things can be bought online, and there are lots of competitors and other salespeople with your product. Live up to the expectation you are putting forth, and exceed it. It is always a good strategy to under promise and over deliver. Treat your client better than you have ever been treated, and they won't ever leave your side.

Gestures go a long way. Use thank you notes, and personalize them. Send birthday and special occasion greetings. Take advantage of social media to send out warm fuzzy affirmations and positive thoughts to your customer base. Send them an email if you saw an article somewhere about something random you discussed. The association with you will become deeper and more meaningful. I knew a banker once who, despite his austere and serious presence, enjoyed sending Valentine's Day cards to all of his customers. He felt it was safe from religious or political associations and sometimes the only Valentine some people would get. It was brilliant and it was surprising! He was extremely successful, by the way!

Everything I've recommended to you so far will help you stand out as a sales professional. Your sense of connection with the client, connecting the client to others, remembering random conversations, expressing gratitude and concern when necessary is all a reflection of how you will take care of the account in the future. Keep up with updates on payments, increases, decreases, and trends in your industry. Contact your clients about things pertaining to their future decision-making when applicable. I always send out a warning when an open enrollment is coming. I send a second warning once it has begun. I send a third warning before it ends. No one can say I didn't keep them informed. It also keeps me fresh in their minds.

This type of relationship is worth nurturing for far more than creating your existing customer's loyalty. It spreads to other aspects of your life. You gain the good will of someone who can be a problem solver in your life too. Perhaps this person is a professional you will need in the future or has a product you might need. Also, this is a person with their own network of friends, family, and associates that will mention you in conversations that arise concerning insurance. You are spreading your business without even knowing it. You might even get invited to speak for audiences you never realized existed.

Chapter 8

CREATE THE BUZZ AND GO-TO PROFESSIONAL REPUTATION

Before presenting at national conferences, I used to pump myself up by thinking, "And now, I'll show them something they've never seen before!" I did, because I have a very creative way of thinking, and I'd build presentations that were unique to me. No one but me could come up with that stuff; I know that for a fact!

It's true of you too! Show the world something they've never seen before! Now it takes preparation and sharp skills in your trade, but if it's you, it's an original!

For those of you who love Shakespeare or literature in general, you know the challenge in storytelling is that there isn't a story that hasn't been told. In many ways, that is true. The basic everyday functions of life are repeated over and over, and all the emotions a human can feel have pretty much been felt. However, it is in the delivery of the story that you share your uniqueness.

Yes, we all know why we need a car. A car gets you from point A to B. It is the ride that counts when you are getting a special car. The reflection of your style, your personality, your activities, or, in my case, dog hair in the back seat. The vehicle you purchase to get you from point A to B is a statement, even if you just want transportation. Utility itself is a statement!

What is the statement you are offering in your presentation of your product? This is your real pitch. People don't buy stuff; they buy a concept or idea. Tap into that. What are you *really* offering?

In the case of insurance, I keep it simple. You are buying financial protection. Now, you might add some other qualities to it, but that's the bottom line. If you don't want to lose your assets during a health crisis or loss, insurance will keep you afloat. Copays, coinsurance, medications, medical supplies, emergency assistance, and other benefits are just an added plus. It's the maximum out of pocket expense that will stop you from bleeding money!

No one has to believe in insurance to find the sense in that statement. They just have to have something to lose and find a solution they are willing to invest in. The details of that will be the creative part and needs analysis.

In finding the right fit, conducting a needs analysis is absolutely crucial. Do not *ever* skip this step. It doesn't have to be long, drawn out, or painful either for you or the client. Be direct and ask why the customer wants insurance. Find out what worries them and what they want to solve with a product. This is how you determine which product the customer needs. Be vigilant.

If I were to present this to a large group, I would present it with images. Images of homes, cars, jewelry, and anything else I believe might be appealing to my audience. Which brings me to my next point.

Know your audience! A church group isn't built the same as a union group or a group of entrepreneurs. Find out about the people gathering to hear you speak and what they value out of what you are presenting. Where are they? What region of the United States or the world do they live in? What elements are they facing day after day? Is it cold? Is it hot? What are their habits? Do members of the group get along or know each other?

Why know so much? The more you know, the more you can connect with your audience. Also, you may have nothing in common with them. Make that statement before they do! Single yourself out as the outsider so no one can hold that against you. Knowing about them will guide you on how to share that information wisely without offending anyone.

Tell them what to think about you before you say anything about your product. A proper introduction will do this, as well as how you stand in front of them. Your name, where you live, and what your journey has been either educationally or professionally to qualify you to speak to them will suffice. A story or anecdote would be appropriate so you can draw them in. It doesn't have to be about you personally. I always made it about my mission. Guess what? It was always their mission!

You will discover that good will is immediate when a goal is shared.

Great, but how do you get in front of an audience? Find groups that hold seminars, discussions, lunch and learns, conferences, and find out how to submit your topic. These proposals take planning and writing skills, but once you get the knack for it, you will find yourself doing a circuit in no time. Chambers of Commerce, professional associations and church groups have speaking events. Look up these types of events in local publications or city websites. Visit a couple of meetings and figure out how to get on their program. Don't forget to multitask and get new business while you are at it!

Now that you have everyone's attention, it is your chance to spread what your mission is too. What is your underlying goal outside of selling a product? What aspect of your buyer's life are you enhancing? Get into the dreams of your audience. How do you want them to picture themselves after the purchase? How will their lives be enhanced?

Know more about your product than just the features and benefits. How does it change lives to know you are covered by insurance? What does true peace of mind mean? Dig deep into the philosophical reason why you are offering anything at all.

Will they be worry-free? Will they be more attractive? Will they attract money, love, and fame? Don't be afraid of this part, because it is the real bait! Remember cigarette ads had people sailing, riding horses, and being rugged cowboys. No matter how many cigarettes you smoke, a sailboat won't appear, and you won't learn how to herd cattle from smoking. It is the emotional association in all advertising, and it works. What will the picture you paint be?

With insurance, the picture is a happy and healthy family enjoying life. Picnics, parties, warm and fuzzy family gatherings are images that will appeal to your audience. A big, safe house with a white picket fence and a loyal dog could also be thrown in. You can get creative with it. If you have a younger crowd, show condos on the beach and water sports. Draw your audience in with images and a promise of something wonderful to associate with your product.

Keep in mind that everyone loves and remembers an original. Don't be the stuffy insurance salesperson people dread to see every year. Once Woody Allen said, "There are worse things in life than death. Have you ever spent an evening with an insurance salesman?" Be a person your clients look forward to seeing and feel comfortable speaking to. Afterall, you are dealing with uncomfortable topics including safety, life, death, and disease. You are guaranteed to run into challenges and obstacles with this subject matter.

Chapter 9

DODGING THE OBSTACLES TO BUILDING A BOOK OF BUSINESS

The method you are learning is strategic selling. It will accumulate clients to your book of sales. With proper attention to detail, you will develop relationship selling, which yields a constant flow of business. However, you may get stuck at any one of the steps. Building a strong, handpicked clientele takes focus.

Identify who needs your product and why they should buy it from you exclusively and no one else. Create a list of who needs what you are selling. Just write it out on a piece of paper. Brainstorm the idea and don't stop.

With each person or profession on the list, identify exactly what that particular customer needs. Why do you think so?

Do some research and find out what your customer's goals are, and discover how you can be instrumental in assuring success. Be sure on how your approach will be, because you want to sound intelligent and knowledgeable about what you are saying. The pitch has to come from the voice of authority.

Then, the most important part is contacting the potential client. Which form of contact will you choose? Will you email, call, or meet at a networking, awards, or social event? Do you know anyone in common who can introduce you? Is there any interest or commonality that you share?

Pursue your clients in a non-invasive way, making them feel at ease and open to learning more about you. Once you meet, don't overwhelm them. Ask to meet over coffee or over lunch. Find out what their availability is and make it something they look forward to. Always accommodate and be open to rescheduling at all times.

Once you are meeting in a comfortable setting and everything is clear, pinpoint how to meet the right people to make the execution of the sale a success without wasting your time and resources. In a kind and polite manner, find out. Who decides what or when to buy? Who has the money? What is the financial situation? Know how to make the financing available if the interest is clearly there. Money should never be an object or obstacle.

Know your competition and what their pricing is. Identify what makes you special above other choices in the market and stand out from the rest. Rate your product and service. Be candid about your choices to represent what you do without bad mouthing others. Why should anyone choose you? Because you are part of the package!

Selling with class and dignity will automatically win everyone's good graces. Be a pleasure to do business with. Even if you are not successful in the first try, you will establish an open-door policy with potential clients for the future. Show them something they've never seen before and get the reputation of being the go-to professional in your circle, which grows your referrals and business leads organically. People talk; what will they say about you?

Every meeting you have and every approach you take will be a topic of conversation, sometimes even over a dinner table that same evening. Remember what Maya Angelou said: "I've learned that people will forget what you said, people will forget what you did, but people will *never forget how you made them feel.*" Be the person that makes everyone you meet feel good.

I'll never forget one of my early mentors, actor Einar Perry Scott, who described someone enchanting an entire room merely by walking into it. This person made everyone in the room feel like they were being embraced in her presence. I immediately wanted to be that person. I learned that it takes a lot of caring and listening to become that charming. Learn to listen and care about what problems your customers have and find the right fit for it with the precision of a NASA engineer or an atom splicer! Your phone will never stop ringing!

Find out where and when you can talk. Get in front of groups of people whenever possible, and draw them to you. Develop your magnetism and draw your audience. How? Know your audience! Find out what they think about and what they want to solve. Repeat all the steps you did when you approached your prospect but do it for a group. All groups share a commonality. Find out what it is and cater to those particular needs. You've got this!

Find conferences and apply to present about interesting topics. The topic should be something innovative and fresh, but also something you know about. Your product should be the solution or something that enhances your presentation. Remember, you will come off as an interesting and extremely intelligent person when you speak about what they are thinking!

If you are afraid of thinking big, think about how fish adapt to the body of water they are in. Years ago, I had a huge pond built for me in my back yard, and I wanted to fill it with Japanese koi fish. At the time, I wasn't making much money as a teacher, and the koi were priced at forty dollars each. So, I went to a local Woolworth's and bought a bag of twenty tiny goldfish for only ninety-nine cents. I spent around a hundred dollars on oxygen producing plants, plants that would hold the fish eggs for their reproduction and other plants for food. So, I created a natural, low maintenance ecosystem in my back yard. Both the fish and plants reproduced at an amazing level and guess what? The tiny goldfish grew to be as big and beautiful as koi.

You can be like one of those tiny goldfish, just find the right pond and grow. Now that you have everyone's attention... *shine!*

Chapter 10

CONTINUE NURTURING AND GROWING A HEALTHY BOOK OF BUSINESS

Congratulations! You have everything you need to move forward and grow your business! This strategy develops the relationships you will need to continue growing your business. The secret to the art of selling is identifying, pursuing, and building relationships. It is by far the most effective way to grow a book of business.

I wrote this book to share what I've learned in all the years I've been in sales and to help you discover joy in selling and personalize it to your own needs and personality. It can be an artform if executed with that intention. It is your choice about how you proceed.

There are many extremely successful salespeople out there that only fill quotas and exploit the vulnerability of the consumer. As much as they seem to be doing well, the harm they do will come back to them when a customer isn't getting the care he or she needs. There are also chargebacks when the issued insurance falls off the books and the harm to your reputation as a problem solver. Basically, you end up losing money!

When you have a relationship with your client, you care about the outcome. As a result, you gain more business when the outcome works out for the client.

Choose clients you will care about and want to cater to. Find them. Meet them. Protect them financially. Become their "respected advisor" for all their insurance needs, and for their families and friends too. Create a situation where they brag about you to others.

The more the relationship and trust grows, the more indispensable you will become to your client.

Identifying desirable clients and pursuing and building relationships is the most effective way to grow a book of business. It will become part of how you experience the world and the people in it. As a result, you will enjoy your life all the better. It won't be a drag to work every day, it will be joyous.

I hope you have enjoyed this process and that it becomes second nature for you.

ACKNOWLEDGMENTS

I'd like to acknowledge my best and closest friends cheering me on along my path, and especially Omar Lopez Chahoud who always told me I should be a writer. Thank you to my dear sister-from-another-mister, Gema Valdes, and her devoted husband Eddie, you are my strength. A shout out to Hilda Hall, my twin born to different parents and a living affirmation of how invincible a woman can be! I also want to thank my former student and forever teacher Jason Stoetzer, a constant source of insight and wealth of wisdom. A final thanks to my special friend Barry Douglass, whose warmth, compassion, and understanding keeps me centered. You are all the constant support system in my life!

A special thanks to Angela Lauria, CEO and founder of The Author Incubator for creating this vehicle for people like me who have been called to write a book and serve. To my developmental editor Ora North and managing editor

Moriah Howell, thanks for making the process an adventurous road to discovery. Many more thanks to everyone else at The Author Incubator, but especially Ramses Rodriguez, Cheyenne Giesecke, and Stacey Warner.

THANK YOU

Thank you for reading my book. I welcome you to participate in my website www.thesecretartofsales.com to share your sales stories. Also, if you would like a more personalized experience, I offer a program that might fit your needs.

Services:
- Personalized sales training tools and content for each service/product.
- Personalized sales playbook and calendar.
- Scheduling and delivering weekly sales skills trainings.
- Building strategies to ensure strong sales results.
- Other related actions as needed.

You can contact me at:
Ana-Maria Figueredo
info@secretartofsales.com
www.secretartofsales.com
305-600-6210

ABOUT THE AUTHOR

Ana-Maria Figueredo is a free-lance writer, award winning educator turned top producing salesperson who has mentored and matched many professionals and artists. She earned a BA in English at FIU with a semester studying British Literature at Cambridge University in England. The same month she graduated, she became a theater, creative writing, and English teacher at Coral Gables High School. She was awarded mention in Who's Who Among America's Teachers multiple times and also won a National Endowment of the Humanities Award to study Plutarch and Ancient Greece at University of Kentucky in Lexington. A few years later, she earned a master's degree in Educational Technology at Barry University.

After leaving her tenure as a classroom teacher, Ana-Maria travelled throughout most of the United States training teachers how to implement technology in the classrooms. She shared her educational implementation techniques in national conferences, which led her to managing the sales for the entire southeast of the country, including Puerto Rico, for various educational software companies. Tired of traveling, during the last ten years, she transferred her technique to insurance sales and has been top producer in various health and life insurance companies. Most recently, she has decided to dedicate herself to her first and ongoing love of writing. Throughout the years, she has written for many blogs, ghost written books, and had a column called "SoBe It" about South Beach, Florida for a dual entrepreneur and philanthropist magazine called DUO.

Ana-Maria writes for many local publications including the *Miami New Times,* and *The Secret Art of Selling Insurance* is her first book. Ana-Maria was born in Brooklyn, New York, but lives in Miami, Florida.

ABOUT DIFFERENCE PRESS

Difference Press is the exclusive publishing arm of The Author Incubator, an educational company for entrepreneurs – including life coaches, healers, consultants, and community leaders – looking for a comprehensive solution to get their books written, published, and promoted. Its founder, Dr. Angela Lauria, has been bringing to life the literary ventures of hundreds of authors-in-transformation since 1994.

A boutique-style self-publishing service for clients of The Author Incubator, Difference Press boasts a fair and easy-to-understand profit structure, low-priced author copies, and author-friendly contract terms. Most importantly, all of our #incubatedauthors maintain ownership of their copyright at all times.

Let's Start a Movement with Your Message

In a market where hundreds of thousands of books are published every year and are never heard from again, The

Author Incubator is different. Not only do all Difference Press books reach Amazon bestseller status, but all of our authors are actively changing lives and making a difference.

Since launching in 2013, we've served over 500 authors who came to us with an idea for a book and were able to write it and get it self-published in less than 6 months. In addition, more than 100 of those books were picked up by traditional publishers and are now available in bookstores. We do this by selecting the highest quality and highest potential applicants for our future programs.

Our program doesn't only teach you how to write a book – our team of coaches, developmental editors, copy editors, art directors, and marketing experts incubate you from having a book idea to being a published, bestselling author, ensuring that the book you create can actually make a difference in the world. Then we give you the training you need to use your book to make the difference in the world, or to create a business out of serving your readers.

Are You Ready to Make a Difference?

You've seen other people make a difference with a book. Now it's your turn. If you are ready to stop watching and start taking massive action, go to http://theauthorincubator.com/apply/.

"Yes, I'm ready!"

---

*Going Home: Saying Goodbye with Grace and Joy
When You Know Your Time is Short*
by Michael G. Giovanni Jr.

*Get Happier, Fitter, and off the Meds Now: 7 Steps to
Improved Health and a Body You Love*
by Ell Graniel

Healed: A Divinely Inspired Path to Healing Cancer
by Pamela Herzer, M.A.

*Live Healthy with Hashimoto's Disease:
The Natural Ayurvedic Approach to Managing
Your Autoimmune Disorder*
by Vikki Hibberd

I Left My Toxic Relationship – Now What?:
The Step-by-Step Guide to Starting over and Living
on Your Own
by Heather J. Kent

Sign Up Your First Coaching Client: Steps
to Launch Your New Career
by Carine Kindinger

Find Your Beloved: Your Guide to Attract True Love
by Rosine Kushnick

My Toddler Has Stopped Having so Many Tantrums:
The Mother's Guide to Finding Joy in Parenting
by Susan Jungermann

In the Eye of a Relationship Storm: Know What
to Do in an Abusive Situation
by Jackquiline Ann

My Clothes Fit Again!: The Overworked Women's
Guide to Losing Weight
by Sue Seal

How Do I Survive?: 7 Steps to Living
after Child Loss
by Patricia Sheveland

*Your Life Matters!: Learn to Write Your Memoir
in 8 Easy Steps*
by Junie Swadron

*Medication Detox: How
to Live Your Best Health, Simplified*
by Rachel Reinhart Taylor M.D.

*Keeping Well: An Anti-Cancer Guide
to Remain in Remission*
by Brittany Wisniewski